50 Pagan Poems

Markle Stermr

50 Pagan Poems

ISBN: 979-8-853-148604

DEDICATION

To the ancestors, my children and my children's
children.

50 Pagan Poems

CONTENTS

50 Pagan Poems

50 Pagan Poems

ACKNOWLEDGMENTS

To each and every one of you who has played a part in this labour of love, I offer my deepest gratitude. May these poems find a place in your hearts as they have in mine.

With love and thanks - Markle

50 Pagan Poems

1. EARTH

In soil and stone, the heart of Earth,
A cradle for life's wondrous birth.
A realm of grounding, steady, true,
Where ancient secrets softly brew.

Beneath the heavens, roots extend,
Through darkness, life and land they mend.
From mountains tall to valleys low,
The element of Earth does grow.

The soil's embrace, a nurturing hold,
Where seeds of hope and dreams unfold.
In every leaf and flower's bloom,
The Earth's rich essence finds its room.

Through changing seasons, cycles turn,
In harmony, her treasures churn.
From shimmering gems to fertile plains,
Her bounty flows in endless reins.

Yet, let us learn, with grateful hearts,
To tread gently where life imparts.
For Earth, a gift of cherished worth,
Deserves our love for all her mirth.

In every step, a bond we share,
With Earth, our home, beyond compare.
With open hearts, we'll find our worth,
For we are bound to this great Earth.

2. AIR

In whispers soft, the zephyrs play,

Through open skies, they gently sway.

A dance unseen, yet felt so near,

The element of air appears.

A fleeting breeze, a sigh of life,

It stirs the trees with gentle strife.

A wisp of clouds, a canvas free,

Painting wonders for all to see.

With every breath, it fills our lungs,

An unseen force, where songs are sung.

In flight, the birds find freedom's call,

Above the world, they soar and sprawl.

From mountaintops to oceans wide,

The winds traverse with boundless pride.

They carry tales of distant lands,

And brush the sand with loving hands.

But heed their might when tempests brew,

For air can rage and fury spew.

Yet even storms, with thunder's boom,

Shall pass away, make way for bloom.

Oh, element of air, so fair,

You touch our lives with tender care.

Through swirling currents, you inspire,

A force of nature we admire.

3. FIRE

In the heart of flames, a dance of light,
The element of Fire burns so bright.
A wild inferno, fierce and bold,
In its embrace, legends unfold.

A force of nature, untamed and free,
It roars with passionate intensity.
From embers small to mighty pyres,
Its warmth and power never tires.

Through darkest nights, it lends its spark,
Guiding lost souls from the dark.
With every flicker, a tale's begun,
Of battles fought and victories won.

Yet, heed its wrath, its untamed rage,
For Fire's fury knows no cage.
In its destructive, untamed desire,
It tests the brave, consuming fire.

But let us seek its wisdom's art,
For Fire can mend and heal the heart.
From its embers, new life is born,
A phoenix rising, love reborn.

Oh, element of Fire, fierce and true,
You teach us strength in all we do.
With courage burning in our core,
We face the world, forevermore.

4. WATER

In gentle ripples or crashing waves,
The element of Water forever misbehaves.
A tranquil stream, a vast ocean's might,
It sustains all living, day and night.

Flowing through valleys, embracing land,
A giver of life, so pure and grand.
From mountain peaks to the ocean's deep,
Its presence, a secret, its treasures keep.

A gentle raindrop, a cleansing shower,
It quenches thirst with its gentle power.
In every tear shed, in joy or sorrow,
Water echoes life's hopes for tomorrow.

A mirror for stars and moon above,
Reflecting wonders, it's born to love.
In its liquid embrace, life's dreams ignite,
A canvas for magic, pure and white.

Yet, Water wields a force untamed,
In storms and floods, it can't be named.
Respect its might, its ebb and flow,
For life and death, it can bestow.

Oh, element of Water, wise and kind,
In unity, our souls are entwined.
From the first drop to the endless sea,
You bind all life, forever free.

5. SPIRIT

In realms unseen, where mysteries lie,

The element of Spirit takes to the sky.

Beyond the tangible, it dances and weaves,

A force of connection that never leaves.

Within our hearts, its ember glows,

Guiding us through highs and lows.

The essence of life, a sacred spark,

In every being, it leaves its mark.

In dreams and visions, it takes flight,

A beacon of hope in the darkest night.

A timeless energy, both near and far,

It binds all souls, like a shining star.

A healer's touch, a poet's song,

In the realm of Spirit, we all belong.

A tapestry woven with threads divine,

Uniting hearts, yours and mine.

In every smile, in every tear,
The element of Spirit draws us near.
With compassion's grace, we find our way,
In unity, we choose to stay.

Oh, element of Spirit, ethereal and pure,
In your embrace, we all endure.
Beyond the bounds of space and time,
You bind our souls, in love's sublime

6. YULE (WINTER SOLSTICE)

In the winter's hush, Yule draws near,
A time of joy, of warmth, and cheer.
As shadows lengthen, nights grow long,
We gather 'round the hearth, a throng.

The solstice comes, the sun's rebirth,
A promise of renewed mirth.
From darkness, light begins to grow,
With every ember's gentle glow.

The Yule log burns, its flames dance high,
A beacon in the wintry sky.
In unity, we celebrate,
The cycle of life, its timeless fate.

With evergreens and holly bright,
We deck the halls on Yuletide night.
A tapestry of love we weave,
A gift to all who dare believe.

With feasts and songs, we honour kin,
Embrace the spirit found within.
In Yule's embrace, our hearts align,
A union of souls, divine.

So let us revel in this grace,
With laughter, love, and warm embrace.
Yule's magic lingers, soft and pure,
A timeless joy, forever sure.

7. IMBOLC (CANDLEMAS)

When winter's chill begins to wane,
And nature stirs from slumber's chain,
Imbolc arrives with hope and light,
A promise of the coming spring's delight.

Brigid's flame, a sacred fire,
Ignites our souls with deep desire.
Her gentle touch, a healer's hand,
Brings forth renewal across the land.

The snowdrops bloom, a pristine white,
A symbol of Imbolc's growing might.
In every bud, a secret birth,
As earth awakens, it reclaims its worth.

With songs and dance, we celebrate,
The turning tides, the changing fate.
The days stretch out, the darkness fade,
As light and life begin to cascade.

The hearth is tended, spirits fed,
In Imbolc's glow, we're safely led.
We bid farewell to winter's sway,
And welcome spring on this sacred day.

So raise your voices, hearts aglow,
In reverence for the earth's ebb and flow.
Imbolc's touch, a gentle art,
A time of hope in every heart.

8. EOSTRE (SPRING EQUINOX)

In the vernal dance of seasons' play,

When winter's grasp begins to sway,

Comes Eostre's festival, pure and bright,

A celebration of life's resplendent flight.

As dawn's first light paints skies in hue,

The earth awakens, born anew.

Eostre's spirit, gentle and free,

Brings hope and love for all to see.

With flowers blooming, colours arrayed,

In nature's arms, we find serenade.

The promise of growth, the promise of birth,

Eostre's blessings, spread across the earth.

In fertile fields and budding trees,

We feel her touch, a gentle breeze.

The eggs she lays, symbols of life,

A tribute to creation's strife.

With joy and laughter, hearts entwine,
In Eostre's circle, souls align.
A time to cherish, a time to share,
Her sacred essence, everywhere.

So as the seasons turn their wheel,
We honour Eostre's presence real.
In harmony with nature's lore,
Her spirit dwells forevermore.

9. BELTANE (MAY DAY)

In Beltane's blaze, the fires ignite,

A sacred dance, a primal rite.

As winter's chill begins to wane,

We hail the spring with joyous refrain.

Upon the hills and fields so green,

The Beltane fires, a sight unseen.

In ribbons, weaved with love and care,

A symbol of the union we declare.

In nature's arms, we come alive,

As Beltane's blessings start to thrive.

The earth responds with fertile grace,

A dance of life in every place.

With maypoles tall, we weave our dreams,

In spirited circles, the laughter screams.

The union of hearts, forever bound,

In Beltane's realm, enchantment found.

In love and passion, spirits soar,

In Beltane's spirit, we explore.

With open hearts and spirits bright,

We honour nature's sacred rite.

So on this day, with joyous cheer,

We welcome Beltane's presence near.

In nature's embrace, we find our way,

To celebrate this blessed day.

10. LITHA (SUMMER SOLSTICE)

As the sun ascends its highest throne,

In Litha's light, we're not alone.

Midsummer's eve, a vibrant dance,

A celebration of life's sweet trance.

The solstice sun, in golden rays,

Illuminates our path and ways.

In nature's bounty, we delight,

As Litha's blessings take their flight.

The meadows bloom, the forests sigh,

Underneath the azure sky.

In every flower, a spark of fire,

A dance of colours, our hearts inspire.

The longest day, the shortest night,

In Litha's embrace, we find delight.

With bonfires blazing, hearts align,

In mirth and magic, spirits entwine.

With friends and kin, we come together,

In love and warmth, forever tethered.

Litha's joy, a gift we treasure,

A time of bliss, a season's pleasure.

So raise a toast, and sing with glee,

To Litha's grace and majesty.

In nature's rhythm, we unite,

In Litha's glow, our souls take flight.

11. LUGNASADH (LAMMAS)

In golden fields, the sun-kissed grain,
Lughnasadh calls, the dancers chain.
As summer's warmth embraces the land,
We gather 'round, a grateful band.

The first fruits ripen, rich and sweet,
Lugh's sacred time, a feast we meet.
With bounteous crops and nature's care,
We honour the harvest, everywhere.

The scythe is raised, the sickle gleams,
In rhythmic dance, we work as teams.
With grateful hearts and hands held high,
We give thanks for the earth and sky.

In every loaf, a labour's pride,
A symbol of the cycle's tide.
The grain transformed through fire's art,
A gift of life to every heart.

With laughter, games, and stories shared,
Lughnasadh's spirit, love declared.
In friendship's circle, spirits blend,
A unity that knows no end.

So as the sun begins to wane,
We celebrate the Lughnasadh's reign.
In nature's cycle, ever true,
A timeless bond, me and you.

12. MABON (AUTUMN EQUINOX)

In Mabon's glow, the days grow mild,
A time of balance, nature's child.
As sun and moon dance side by side,
We find the grace in life's ebb and tide.

The harvest moon, a golden sphere,
Sheds light on fields, both far and near.
In gratitude, we gather around,
For nature's gifts that do abound.

The apples sweet, the grapes divine,
In Mabon's bounty, we entwine.
With blessings shared, hearts overflow,
In unity, our spirits grow.

A tapestry of russet hues,
The changing leaves, a vibrant muse.
In nature's art, we find our way,
Through cycles that forever sway.

In twilight's hour, we take a breath,

Embracing life's sweet dance till death.

In Mabon's realm, we pause to see,

The beauty in life's tapestry.

So let us cherish this sacred time,

In Mabon's rhythm, hearts align.

With gratitude and love profound,

In harmony, we're forever bound.

13. SAMHAIN (HALLOWEEN)

When autumn's hues adorn the land,
And shadows lengthen, hand in hand,
Comes Samhain, a sacred night,
A time of magic, dark and light.

Beneath the moon's bewitching glow,
The veils between the worlds grow thin, we know,
Where spirits roam and whispers wane,
A dance of mystic realms regain.

The harvest's bounty, rich and sweet,
We share with kin in warmth and heat.
As bonfires blaze, the embers fly,
Old tales and songs fill the sky.

Ancestral spirits softly call,
Their wisdom echoes in the thrall,
Of drums that beat, and candles' flame,
In reverence, we speak their name.

With pumpkin lanterns glowing bright,
We ward off darkness through the night.
A time to honour those now passed,
Their presence felt, a love that lasts.

So, gather close, hearts intertwine,
Embrace the ancient, the divine.
In Samhain's grasp, we find the way,
To welcome winter's whispered stay.

14. DRUIDRY

Amidst the ancient woods, a wisdom thrives,

Where Druidry weaves its mystic lives.

A sacred path, in harmony with earth,

Through cycles spun, where nature finds its worth.

In reverence to the moon and stars above,

Druids seek the secrets of the Grove.

With oaken staff and mistletoe,

They walk the land, with spirits they go.

Through sacred rites, the seasons turn,

In sacred circles, souls discern.

A dance of light and shadow's play,

In Druidry's embrace, we find our way.

With cauldrons stirred and chants well-sung,

The old ways echo, forever young.

In every leaf, a whispered prayer,

To honour life and love so rare.

For in the heart of Druid's creed,

A deeper truth, a sacred seed.

A kinship bound with land and sky,

In Druidry's embrace, we unify.

With every dawn, a timeless art,

A bond with nature, mind, and heart.

Through Druidry's light, we strive to see,

The interconnected web of all that be.

15. GOLDEN SICKLE

In ancient groves where secrets sleep,
A Druid's heart its vigil keeps.
With golden sickle, gleaming bright,
They tend to nature's sacred rite.

Beneath the moon's enchanting gleam,
They harvest dreams like sacred beams.
With gentle touch and reverence deep,
The sickle's blade, their vows they keep.

In sacred rites of sun and rain,
The Druid's sickle knows no stain.
With every stroke, a bond they weave,
With earth and sky, they interleave.

Through cycles spun, the seasons turn,
With golden sickle's grace discern.
A symbol of the harvest's might,
In Druid's hand, a shining light.

In nature's dance, the sickle's swung,
A melody through realms unsung.
With each harvest, a sacred gift,
The Druid's golden sickle lift.

So in the heart of ancient lore,
The sickle's gold forever more.
A cherished tool, their hearts aglow,
In Druid's hand, a legacy to grow.

16. WICCA

In sacred circles, beneath the moon's glow,
The Wiccans gather, their spirits aglow.
A tapestry woven with magic's might,
They honour nature, both day and night.

With reverence for earth, air, fire, and sea,
In harmony, they live, wild and free.
With herbs and crystals, their spells they weave,
To heal, to guide, and to believe.

Through cycles of seasons, they find their way,
Embracing the light and the dark in play.
With pentagrams and candles alight,
They dance with the elements through the night.

In tune with the stars and the cosmic sky,
They seek ancient wisdom, not asking why.
The goddess and god, a divine embrace,
In Wiccan's heart, they find their sacred space.

In love and respect for all life's forms,

They cherish the earth through tempests and storms.

A path of love, compassion, and light,

In Wiccans' hearts, the magic takes flight.

17. SACRED ATHAME

In the realm of mystic lore, a blade of old,
An athame gleams, its secrets yet untold.
A sacred tool, a witch's guiding light,
In shadows cast, it dances through the night.

With hilt adorned, a handle firm and strong,
It holds the essence of the earth's sweet song.
A conduit for the energy we weave,
A symbol of the power we receive.

In rituals and circles, it takes its place,
A guardian of the sacred sacred space.
With incantations whispered soft and true,
It channels energies, both old and new.

A symbol of the goddess and the god,
The athame points to realms we gently trod.
With every blade, a connection found,
To ancient wisdom, to the sight profound.

A bond of trust, a bond of sacred trust,

In reverence, we hold the blade we must.

For in its edge, a balance we attain,

A sacred athame, forever we retain.

18. HEATHENRY

Beneath the sky of Northern lands,

Where ancient tales and myths expand,

Heathenry dwells, a sacred lore,

In reverence for the gods of yore.

In the halls of Valhalla's might,

Where warriors rest in endless light,

The Heathens seek ancestral bond,

With Odin's wisdom far beyond.

With Mjölnir's strength and Freyja's grace,

They honour gods in every place.

Through blizzards fierce and summers fair,

The Heathens find their spirits rare.

With sacred symbols carved in wood,

The runes of old, a guide they stood.

In nature's embrace, they find their way,

Through twilight's dance and dawning day.

Respect for land, for sea, for sky,
In Heathenry's heart, they unify.
A kinship strong, like roots entwined,
A legacy of ancient kind.

Through fireside tales and sacred rites,
They keep the flame of faith ignites.
With love for land and ancestors' song,
In Heathen's heart, they do belong.

19. HEATHEN RITUAL STAFF

In Northern lands where Heathens roam,
A ritual staff finds sacred home.
Carved from the heart of ancient trees,
It holds the essence of mysteries.

In runes and symbols etched with care,
A staff of power, beyond compare.
In Heathen's hand, a beacon bright,
Guiding through day and dark of night.

With Thor's strength and Freyja's grace,
The staff invokes the gods' embrace.
Through blizzards fierce or summer's fair,
It weaves a bond with earth and air.

In rituals held 'neath moon and stars,
The staff connects to realms afar.
With every step, a journey starts,
Guided by its ancient arts.

A symbol of the old and wise,

The Heathen's staff, a treasured prize.

Through sacred rites and chants they sing,

Its presence brings a sacred ring.

With every touch, the worlds align,

In Heathen's ritual, they find

A connection to their ancestral past,

Through the staff's power, steadfast.

20. OGHAM

In ancient script of Ogham's grace,
The trees reveal their sacred trace.
Carved on stones or etched in wood,
Their wisdom speaks through ages stood.

Each symbol holds a tale untold,
In nature's language, truths unfold.
From birch to oak, the forest's lore,
In Ogham's script, we seek and explore.

A secret code of ancient bards,
In every line, their voice regards.
Through winding strokes and marks aligned,
The Ogham whispers, intertwined.

With druid's hand, the message weaves,
From cradle of oak to sea's soft leaves.
In sacred groves and twilight's hush,
Ogham's chant, a mystic rush.

A guide for seekers, brave and wise,

Through Ogham's script, their spirits rise.

In every letter, magic's breath,

Ogham's song, a dance of death.

So let us listen, hearts laid bare,

In Ogham's script, we find our share.

In nature's embrace, we stand tall,

With Ogham's song, we heed the call.

21. RUNES

In ancient script, on stones of old,

The Runes' tale, a story told.

Carved with wisdom, etched with might,

They carry secrets through the night.

Each symbol holds a mystic key,

A glimpse of fate, a destiny.

In patterns formed, their magic weaves,

Through whispers carried by the leaves.

From ancient tribes to modern minds,

The Runes' wisdom intertwines.

With Odin's eye, they see beyond,

In sacred dance, their power spawned.

In divination, they impart,

The guidance of the elder's heart.

With every cast, a rune's insight,

A pathway through both day and night.

In twilight's realm, their essence gleams,

The Runes' light, a waking dream.

In nature's pulse, their energy,

The Runes' song, a legacy.

So let us listen, hearts laid bare,

To Runes' whispers in the air.

In ancient script, their wisdom shared,

The Runes' gift, forever cared.

22. SCRYING

In twilight's haze, a mystic art,

Scrying's realm, where visions start.

Through crystal's gaze or mirror's sheen,

A window to the unseen.

The seer's eye, a sacred sight,

Beyond the veil of day and night.

In whispers soft, the future weaves,

Through Scrying's dance, the soul perceives.

In darkened room, the candles' glow,

The seer's heart begins to know.

With focused mind and spirit's grace,

They seek the truths of time and space.

Reflections ripple, water's dance,

The Scryer's trance, a mystic trance.

In symbols formed, the depths disclose,

A tapestry of fate's repose.

Through crystal ball or polished stone,

The Scrying art, a journey's flown.

In ancient craft, the seer's might,

Unravelling mysteries of the night.

So let us peer with open mind,

In Scrying's realm, answers we find.

A sacred practice, tried and true,

The seer's gift, a cosmic view.

23. ASTROLOGY

In starlit skies, where wonders lie,

Astrology unveils the cosmic tie.

Through zodiac's embrace and planetary dance,

The heavens whisper their cosmic trance.

Aries' fire, bold and bright,

Taurus' strength, an earthly might.

Gemini's twins, duality's play,

Cancer's nurture, like the bay.

Leo roars with regal grace,

Virgo's touch, a tender trace.

Libra seeks balance, fair and just,

Scorpio delves in passions' thrust.

Sagittarius, an archer's aim,

Capricorn climbs to heights of fame.

Aquarius' water, a free spirit's call,

Pisces dreams in mystic thrall.

With birth charts drawn, the stars align,
Astrology weaves its grand design.
A celestial map, a guiding chart,
Revealing patterns of the heart.

In cosmic cycles, we find our way,
Astrology's wisdom lights the day.
Through moon and sun, the planets' sway,
In astro's gaze, we learn and pray.

So let us ponder, seek the signs,
In Astrology's realm, the divine.
A language written in the skies,
Connecting souls, as time defies.

24. ASTRAL PLANING

In twilight's realm, where dreams take flight,

Spiritual Astral planing ignites.

Beyond the bounds of earthly plane,

Our souls ascend, no bounds restrain.

With astral wings, we journey far,

To realms of stars, where mysteries are.

Through cosmic paths, our spirits roam,

In astral planes, we find our home.

In meditation's gentle sway,

Our astral selves begin to play.

Through veils of time, we travel free,

To seek the truths that set us free.

In sacred space, our consciousness,

Explores the realms of vastness.

In unity with cosmic grace,

Our astral journeys we embrace.

So in the astral realms, we soar,

Infinite possibilities in store.

With spirit's guide, we'll safely roam,

Through astral planes, our souls shall roam.

25. MAIDEN, MOTHER AND CRONE

In cycles three, the phases unfold,

The Maiden, the Mother, and the Crone, we're told.

With youth's embrace, the Maiden's grace,

In spring's embrace, she finds her place.

In summertime, the Mother reigns,

With nurturing love, her heart sustains.

With life's creation, she's endowed,

A sacred bond, forever vowed.

In autumn's glow, the Crone appears,

Her wisdom deep, through countless years.

The harvest's bounty, she'll bestow,

As seasons turn, her knowledge grow.

Through Maiden, Mother, and Crone's dance,

The wheel of life continues its advance.

Each phase a gift, a sacred role,

In nature's rhythm, we find our soul.

For in this trinity's embrace,

The Maiden, the Mother, and the Crone, we trace,

The essence of the woman's art,

A timeless dance of love and heart.

26. THE MORRIGAN

In Celtic lore, a goddess reigns,
The Morrigan, where darkness wanes.
A triad queen of mysteries deep,
In battles fierce, her secrets keep.

With raven's wing and warrior's might,
She soars above the field of fight.
In war's embrace, her presence known,
A harbinger of fate is shown.

In times of change, her voice is near,
The Morrigan, with wisdom clear.
Her prophecy, a guiding light,
A guardian through day and night.

In death's domain, she weaves her thread,
Among the spirits of the dead.
A psychopomp, her role defined,
Guiding souls to realms divine.

But in her realm, where shadows dwell,
A nurturing side she'll often tell.
For as the crone, she holds life's key,
In cycles spun eternally.

So in The Morrigan's ancient art,
We find her strength in every heart.
In darkness and in light, she thrives,
A goddess fierce, forever alive.

27. KING LUGH

In Celtic realms, a hero's tale,
Lugh's legend, like the wind, sets sail.
A master of crafts, a warrior's might,
He shines like the sun, forever bright.

With spear in hand and skills refined,
Lugh's talents, a celestial find.
A champion of skill and art,
In every contest, he played his part.

A harvest god, his blessings pour,
Abundance blooms forevermore.
In fields and meadows, his touch is felt,
The fruits of labor, richly dealt.

As summer's king, his reign extends,
A time of joy, where laughter blends.
With games and mirth, his name resounds,
In Lugh's embrace, life's dance abounds.

So in the echoes of his fame,

We honour Lugh's immortal name.

A deity of light and might,

His legacy, forever bright.

28. HECATE

In shadows deep, where mysteries reside,

Hecate, the goddess, stands with pride.

A triple form, a trinity's embrace,

In her domain, all worlds interlace.

With crescent moon, her crown of night,

She guides lost souls towards the light.

In crossroads' maze, her torches gleam,

Illuminating paths unseen.

As mistress of the dark and wild,

Her wisdom's depth, like the ocean's tide.

A sorceress, with cauldron's art,

She stirs the brew of life's grand chart.

In ancient rites, her presence felt,

A guardian of the veil that melts.

Through life and death, her realm extends,

A guiding hand, on fate she bends.

So in the embrace of Hecate's might,

We find our strength, our inner sight.

In moonlit dance, we praise her name,

Hecate, the goddess, eternal flame.

29. FRIGG

In halls of Asgard, where gods reside,

Frigg, the queen, with grace and pride.

Wife of Odin, wise and fair,

With love and care, she fills the air.

A goddess of hearth and home, she reigns,

Her embrace, a warmth that never wanes.

With mother's touch and lover's kiss,

She nurtures all, in blissful bliss.

As guardian of fate's tangled thread,

Her knowledge vast, by few is fed.

The weaver of destinies entwined,

Her wisdom's web, forever bind.

In skies above, her ravens soar,

With messages that she'll implore.

A goddess fierce, and yet serene,

Frigg's presence, a living dream.

So in her grace, we find our way,

In Frigg's embrace, we choose to stay.

A guiding light through day and night,

Her love, a beacon burning bright.

30. ODIN

In realms of ancient myths and lore,
Odin, the All-Father, we adore.
With wisdom's eye and raven's wing,
He soars above, a godly king.

In battle's heat, a warrior bold,
His spear's thrust, a tale retold.
A seeker of knowledge, vast and wide,
He sacrificed to gain insights inside.

With one eye lost, but vision clear,
He sought the wisdom, without fear.
In runes and magic, he excelled,
The secrets of the Norns he held.

A wanderer of realms unseen,
In search of truths that lie between.
To Valhalla's hall, the brave he'd call,
A valiant host, standing tall.

A wanderer of realms unseen,
In search of truths that lie between.

To Valhalla's hall, the brave he'd call,
A valiant host, standing tall.

So in the tales of Odin's reign,
We find his wisdom, not in vain.
A god of strength and knowledge's might,
Odin, the All-Father, a guiding light.

31. THOR

In thunder's roar and lightning's might,
Thor, the god of strength and light.
With Mjölnir's swing, the sky he rends,
Protector of Asgard, he defends.

A warrior's heart, so brave and bold,
In battles fought, his tales are told.
With golden locks and eyes of blue,
In Thor's embrace, the brave are true.

The storms may rage, but he stands tall,
The might of thunder, at his call.
In Odin's hall, his seat is found,
A hero's strength, forever renowned.

With friends he feasts, a boisterous cheer,
In tales and mead, their bond is clear.
Yet when dark foes threaten the land,
Thor's hammer strikes, a mighty hand.

So in the myths of days of yore,

Thor's legend lives forevermore.

A god of thunder, fierce and grand,

In Asgard's realm, he'll ever stand.

32. FREYJA

In fields of gold where flowers bloom,
Freyja's grace, a radiant gloom.
With falcon cloak and chariot's flight,
Goddess of love, she shines so bright.

A warrior's heart, a lover's embrace,
Freyja's presence, a sacred space.
In battle fierce or love's sweet hold,
Her spirit weaves, both fierce and bold.

With amber tears and golden charms,
She enchants all in her arms.
In Brísingamen's gleam, her worth,
Freyja, the goddess of love and mirth.

In fields of Folkvangr, she'll reign,
A leader fierce, a queen's domain.
Her cats and boar, her loyal kin,
In her embrace, they'll ever spin.

So in the Northern skies above,

Freyja's essence, forever love.

A goddess strong, in tales divine,

Her legacy, for all of time.

33. CERIDWEN

In cauldron's brew, where magic stirs,
Ceridwen weaves her spells, a blur.
With ancient wisdom, eyes aglow,
She holds the secrets, high and low.

A mother goddess, fierce and kind,
In moonlit nights, her presence bind.
Through darkened woods and starry skies,
Ceridwen's essence, never dies.

Her cauldron's depths, a womb of life,
A potion's birth, through strife and strife.
In transformative, potent art,
She stirs the brew, a brand new start.

In Celtic lore, her tale unfolds,
A sorceress of stories old.
With poetic gift, her gifts she'll share,
Ceridwen's presence, ever rare.

So in the whispers of the breeze,

Ceridwen's spirit, we do seize.

A goddess wise, with love embraced,

In every heart, her magic placed.

34. TALIESIN

In bardic verse, a legend's birth,

Taliesin's words, a spell on Earth.

With gifted lyre and wisdom's gleam,

He weaves his tales, a timeless dream.

From cauldron's brew to ancient lore,

Taliesin's spirit soars and soars.

In Awen's flow, his muse takes flight,

His verses dance in moonlit light.

A poet's heart, a seer's sight,

Taliesin's gift, a guiding light.

Through trials faced and journeys long,

His courage sings a warrior's song.

In Arthur's court, his presence known,

His words, a power brightly shown.

With every tale and ballad's flow,

Taliesin's legacy shall grow.

So in the echoes of his rhyme,

Taliesin's spirit stands through time.

A bardic soul, forever free,

In every verse, his truth we see.

35. PENTAGRAM / PENTACLE

In sacred circles, it takes its stand,

The pentagram, a symbol so grand.

With five points linked, in harmony,

The Pagan's emblem of unity.

Each point representing elements true,

Earth, Air, Fire, Water, and Spirit's view.

In ritual's dance, it's drawn with care,

A symbol of power, a symbol so rare.

The pentacle, a disk of might,

An altar's tool, reflecting light.

Inscribed with symbols, ancient and old,

Its magick weaves, a story told.

Within its grasp, energies align,

In sacred space, intentions shine.

A connection to the divine's embrace,

The pentagram's power, forever in place.

With every point, a world's embrace,

The Pagan's path, a sacred chase.

Through pentagram and pentacle's sight,

They find their truth, their inner light.

36. CASTING A CIRCLE

In sacred space, with hearts aligned,
We cast a circle, powers entwined.
With candles' glow and incense rise,
The circle forms before our eyes.

With athame's touch and wand's command,
We weave a barrier, firm and grand.
A boundary strong, a space between,
The mundane world and realms unseen.

In clockwise motion, we proceed,
Intentions set, with love and heed.
In sacred words, we call the four,
Earth, Air, Fire, Water's lore.

With every step, the energy grows,
Within the circle's sacred throes.
A vortex of magick, swirling wide,
Our intentions soar, side by side.

In circle's grace, we chant and dance,
As spirits join in the sacred trance.
Connected now, as one we stand,
United in this mystic land.

Within the circle's hallowed space,
We find our power, our soul's embrace.
With gratitude and hearts aglow,
In unity, our magick flows.

So as we cast the circle's might,
We honour nature's sacred light.
In harmony with earth and sky,
We bid the circle's energy goodbye.

37. SPIRIT GUIDES

In shadows' veil, where spirits glide,
Spirit guides, forever by our side.
With wisdom's touch, they gently steer,
In whispers soft, our hearts they hear.

Ancestral souls or beings bright,
They guide us through both day and night.
In dreams they come, in signs they show,
Their presence felt, a loving glow.

Through trials faced and paths unknown,
Spirit guides, our hearts are sown.
In sacred trust, their guidance true,
They light the way, our souls renew.

With every step, they walk with grace,
A bond of love, they won't erase.
In unity, our souls align,
With spirit guides, a love divine.

So in the silence of our hearts,

We'll feel their presence, ne'er to part.

Spirit guides, a cherished friend,

In their embrace, our journey's mend.

38. CASTING A SPELL

In sacred circle, whispers rise,

As mystic words begin to size.

With focused mind and heart's desire,

We cast a spell, our spirits higher.

With candles' glow and incense's scent,

Our intentions strong, their energy spent.

Herbs and crystals, symbols weave,

In magick's dance, our dreams receive.

With wand or athame, we direct,

The spell's intent, its purpose select.

Through ancient arts, we weave and blend,

The elements' might, to comprehend.

In harmony with moon and star,

We cast the spell, near or far.

With sacred chant and focused will,

Our magick's essence, we fulfill.

A cycle's turn, a circle's round,

In spellwork's power, we are bound.

With gratitude, we set it free,

The spell is cast, so mote it be.

39. POPPETS

In witch's hands, a poppet's found,
A symbol of the magic bound.
With herbs and thread, its form takes shape,
A tool of power, a spell to drape.

A tiny figure, made with care,
In likeness of the one we bear.
With intention set, it holds the key,
To weave our wishes, wild and free.

Through moonlit nights and daylight's gleam,
The poppet works its subtle scheme.
With pins and charms, its purpose true,
In sacred trust, our dreams pursue.

With every stitch, a bond's embrace,
A poppet's magick, interlace.
In love and healing, harm's dispel,
Its potent charm, a mystic spell.

So in the hands of witches old,

The poppets work, their power unfold.

With love and light, their spirits high,

Through witch's hands, the poppets fly.

40. CANDLE MAGICK

By candle's flame, in flickering light,
Witch's magick takes its flight.
With colours chosen, intentions set,
The spell begins, no bounds to fret.

In sacred space, the candles glow,
Their energy begins to flow.
Through incantations, whispered clear,
The witch's power draws near.

Each candle holds a mystic hue,
A symbol of the magick's brew.
With focused mind and heart aligned,
The witch's spell, forever bind.

In moonlit dance and starry night,
The candle's glow, a beacon bright.
Through witch's hands, the energy's spun,
In candle magick, a dance is done.

With ancient arts, the witches craft,
Their spells, a legacy that will last.
Through candle's flame, intentions rise,
In witch's magick, we realize.

So in the witch's candle's dance,
A spell is woven, a sacred chance.
With love and light, their spirits soar,
Through candle magick, evermore.

41. CRYSTAL MAGICK

In crystals' embrace, the witches find,
A magick realm, both pure and kind.
With stones of power, each one unique,
Their energies, a mystic clique.

Through amethyst and quartz's gleam,
The witches' visions start to stream.
In sacred space, their spirits soar,
In crystal magick, they'll explore.

With moonstone's glow and citrine's hue,
Their intentions strong, they imbue.
In harmony with earth and sky,
Their crystal magick starts to fly.

Through crystal grids and sacred chants,
The witches' spell, the universe grants.
With crystal allies, side by side,
Their magickal forces now reside.

With every facet, every gleam,

The witches' dreams become a theme.

In crystal magick's radiant art,

Their spirits soar, their souls take part.

So in the witches' crystal dance,

A spell is cast, a sacred trance.

In love and light, their power swells,

Through crystal magick's ancient spells.

42. MOON MAGICK

Beneath the silver moon's embrace,

Wiccan magick finds its place.

In phases waxing, full, and waning,

The moon's allure, forever reigning.

With lunar cycles, witches weave,

Their spells of love, of hope, believe.

In sacred circle, they unite,

To harness moonbeams' gentle light.

Through incantations softly spoken,

Their wishes sent, their spirits woken.

With moon's enchantment, dreams they chase,

In Wiccan moon magick's sacred space.

From crescent sliver to orb so round,

The moon's energy, they surround.

In every phase, a spell's desire,

Their intentions set, the moon shall inspire.

So in the moonlit hours, they roam,

In Wiccan moon magick, they find home.

A dance with cosmos, spirits high,

Beneath the moonlit, starry sky.

43. FAMILIARS I

In mystic realms where spirits roam,
Wiccan familiars find their home.
An animal guide, a sacred bond,
Their presence felt, their hearts respond.

In moonlit woods and shadows deep,
Their energy, a secret keep.
With knowing eyes, they see unseen,
A Wiccan's soul, they'll e'er convene.

Through whispers soft and paw's embrace,
A familiar's love, we'll ne'er replace.
In magick's dance, they'll stand beside,
A faithful companion, by our side.

With intuition, keen and bright,
They guide us through both day and night.
Through ancient wisdom, they impart,
A Wiccan's familiars, heart to heart.

So in the circle's sacred grace,

We honour familiars' ancient place.

A bond with spirits, wild and true,

A Wiccan's familiars, forever new.

44. FAMILIARS II

In the sacred bond, witches find,
Familiars true, their hearts aligned.
With spirits kind and eyes that gleam,
Together they'll weave a mystic dream.

Be it cat or owl, or toad or crow,
A familiar's love, forever shall grow.
In whispers shared and knowing gaze,
Their connection deep, a timeless maze.

Through moonlit nights and twilight's kiss,
Familiars guide with gentle bliss.
In witch's circle, they stand tall,
Protectors true, through rise and fall.

A friend, a guide, a source of power,
In familiars' eyes, secrets tower.
In nature's realm, they dance and play,
A trusted partner, night and day.

So in the witch's heart and soul,

A familiar's presence makes them whole.

Together they'll journey through the night,

In Wiccan magic's sacred light.

45. ANCESTOR WORSHIP

In the whispers of the ancient past,
Ancestor worship's bonds hold fast.
With reverence deep, their spirits soar,
Through generations, forever more.

In sacred rituals, we connect,
To those whose blood in us reflects.
Their wisdom echoes through the years,
A guiding light, dispelling fears.

Through stories told and memories shared,
Ancestors' love is always bared.
Their strength and courage, we embrace,
In their presence, we find grace.

With offerings given, hearts entwine,
Ancestor worship's flame divine.
In gratitude for paths they paved,
Their legacy, forever engraved.

So in the circle of life's embrace,

We honour ancestors' rightful place.

With love and respect, our hearts unite,

In their presence, we find our light.

46. NATURE WORSHIP

In sacred groves, where oak trees stand,

Druid nature worship takes its hand.

With reverence deep, they seek to find,

The spirits of the earth entwined.

Through sunrise's kiss and moon's embrace,

Druids honour nature's grace.

In every leaf, a story told,

Their hearts and souls forever bold.

With whispers soft, the winds convey,

The wisdom of each passing day.

In harmony with land and sky,

Druids' spirits soar so high.

The rivers' flow, a sacred dance,

The essence of life's grand expanse.

In nature's rhythm, they align,

With every creature, every pine.

With bards' song and druids' prayer,

The spirits of the earth they bear.

In ancient ways, their hearts embrace,

The gifts of nature's boundless space.

So in the realm of Druid's lore,

Their nature worship, they adore.

In every breath, their love's displayed,

For Mother Earth, their hearts are swayed.

47. MOTHER EARTH

In verdant fields where life takes birth,
Mother Earth, the womb of mirth.
With gentle touch and nurturing grace,
She cradles life in her embrace.

From mountains high to oceans wide,
Her beauty's breadth, a boundless tide.
In forests deep and meadows green,
Her wonders are forever seen.

Through seasons' turn, her cycles flow,
In harmony with moon's soft glow.
With every dawn and twilight's sigh,
Her spirit breathes, the land and sky.

With each breath we take, we're blessed,
By Mother Earth's eternal nest.
In her care, we find our worth,
Forever bound to Mother Earth.

48 SHAPE SHIFTING

Amidst the ancient oak and misty glade,
Druidic shapeshifting's power displayed.
In whispered rites beneath the moon's gaze,
They journey through a timeless maze.

With primal call and nature's force,
The Druid's spirit takes its course.
Through chants and herbs, they transform,
Embracing beasts in wild life's swarm.

A wolf's keen eye, a falcon's flight,
In shapeshifting's dance, they find delight.
From human form to creature's guise,
Their spirits soar, no limits to size.

Through shrouded veils and secret arts,
The Druid's essence freely departs.
With kinship bound to all life's forms,
They honour nature in all its norms.

So in the heart of Druid's creed,

Shapeshifting's mysteries intercede.

A bond with creatures, wild and free,

In Druidic shapeshifting's decree.

49. ARWEN

In sacred groves where Druids meet,
Their chanting voices, pure and sweet.
Arwen, Arwen, Arwen's name,
Resounds like nature's gentle flame.

In harmony, their voices rise,
Beneath the moon and starlit skies.
With ancient words and mystic tone,
They weave a spell, their hearts intone.

Arwen, Arwen, Arwen's grace,
A chant that time cannot erase.
Through forest's embrace, their song is heard,
A sacred hymn, a whispered word.

With every note, a bond they find,
To nature's realm, their souls aligned.
Arwen, Arwen, Arwen's call,
In Druidic chanting, spirits enthrall.

So in the circle of their rite,

Arwen's name, a beacon bright.

In harmony with Earth and sky,

Their chanting echoes, spirits fly.

50. AVALON

In legends told of days of old,

Avalon's isle, with secrets untold.

A realm of beauty, a mystical shore,

Where Arthur rests forevermore.

In veiled mists and shimmering light,

Avalon's magic takes its flight.

A healing place, where wounds mend,

A sanctuary, where spirits ascend.

With Lady of the Lake's guiding hand,

Excalibur found in sacred sand.

In Avalon's realm, a king's reprieve,

Arthur's spirit, forever believe.

Through ancient tales, the whispers run,

Of Avalon's glory beneath the sun.

A place of wonder, where legends lie,

In Arthurian Avalon, dreams won't die.

ABOUT THE AUTHOR

Markle, the creative mind behind this collection of poems, is an avid wordsmith and an ardent lover of the written art. From the early days of scribbling thoughts in journals to weaving verses that dance on the page, writing has been a steadfast companion on Markle's journey.

Printed in Great Britain
by Amazon